Accounting comparisons

UK, Belgium, Italy & Spain

Accounting comparisons

UK, Belgium, Italy & Spain

Compiled by Christopher Nobes
Coopers & Lybrand Professor of Accounting
University of Reading

London, 1997

This book aims to provide general guidance only and does not purport to deal with all possible questions and issues which may arise in any given situation. Should the reader encounter particular problems he is advised to seek professional advice, which Coopers & Lybrand would be pleased to provide.

No responsibility for loss occasioned to any person acting or refraining from action as a result of any material in this publication can be accepted by the author, copyright owner or publisher.

Coopers & Lybrand is authorised by the Institute of Chartered Accountants in England and Wales to carry on investment business.

ISBN 1 85355 814 1

© Coopers & Lybrand, UK
October 1997

Printed and bound in Great Britain by
Progressive Printing (UK) Ltd, Essex

All rights reserved. No part of this publication may be reproduced, stored in any retrieval system, or transmitted in any form or by any means, electronic, mechanical, photocopying, recording, or otherwise, without the prior permission of Coopers & Lybrand, UK.

Foreword

As the representative organisation for the accountancy profession in Europe, grouping together 38 member bodies in 26 countries, including all European Union Member States and four Central and Eastern European countries, FEE (Fédération des Experts Comptables Européens) attaches great importance to comparative accounting research on a pan-European basis. One of our main objectives is to work towards the enhancement and harmonisation of accountancy in the broadest sense in Europe in both the public and private sectors, and this can only be done on the basis of an understanding of the differences which currently exist.

With this goal in mind, FEE itself has undertaken several major projects, the most recent of which have included *Bank Accounts Directive Options and their Implementation, Accounting Treatment of Financial Instruments – A European Perspective, Research Paper on Expert Statements in Environmental Reports* and most recently the *FEE Comparative Study on Conceptual Frameworks in Europe*. The latter concludes that there is a need to understand and to solve accounting inconsistencies on a conceptual level in Europe. Without a framework, it will be difficult to find the right solutions.

We welcome this third edition of this book in the successful series Accounting Comparisons. These publications have contributed to an improved understanding of divergences in the financial reporting in Europe, and are therefore an additional step towards improving the comparability of European financial statements.

David Darbyshire
President
Fédération des Experts Comptables Européens (FEE)

Preface

This book is part of a series on the subject of international accounting comparisons. This is the third edition of this volume, which covers the UK, Belgium, Italy and Spain. It is updated for changes up to early 1997.

As will be shown throughout this book, there are major accounting differences between the countries examined here, although these have diminished as member countries have implemented the EU Company Law Directives. The differences cause difficulties for investors, management, auditors and others who operate internationally. It is hoped that the information contained here will help the reader to begin the process of understanding and adjusting for the international differences.

This series uses UK practices as the basis for comparison, principally because London is the major financial centre in Europe, particularly in terms of the numbers of publicly traded companies. Further, many other countries may find a UK benchmark the easiest European one to work from. This is likely to be the case for Commonwealth countries, and for the US and countries that are familiar with US practices. The same point applies to the choice of English as the uniform language for the book, except of course for the glossary. The use of a UK benchmark enables the series of books to be used together.

This book is not intended to be a detailed practice manual for preparers or auditors of accounts. It is not exhaustive and it frequently deals particularly with large or listed companies. It is *not* designed to cover specialist companies such as banks or insurance companies. Furthermore, change is very rapid in accounting in Europe. As a result, some parts of the book may have become outdated since publication.

I am particularly grateful for advice received from colleagues, including Eddy Dams (Brussels), GA Delucchi (Milan) and Antonio Pulido Alvarez (Madrid).

Preface

Enquiries concerning the contents of this book should be addressed to any office of the member firms of Coopers & Lybrand Europe. The addresses of some principal offices and a list of locations in Europe are given at the end of this book.

Christopher Nobes

University of Reading
October 1997

Contents

	Page
Foreword	v
Preface	vii

Chapter

1 **Setting the scene** 1
    The background to European accounting 1
    EU harmonisation 5

2 **Companies, publication, audit and formats** 9
    Companies 9
    Publication and audit 11
    Other general accounting features 13
    Accounting for changing prices 13
        Accounting policy changes 13
        Prior period adjustments 13
        Post balance sheet events 14
    Related party transactions 14
    Formats 14

3 **Valuation of assets** 17
    Principles of valuation 17
    Tangible fixed assets 18
    Intangibles 19
    Investments 20
    Stocks 21
    Debtors and creditors 22
    Contingencies 23
    Reserves and provisions 23

4 **Measurement of profit** 25
    Principles of measurement 25
    Depreciation 25
    Deferred tax 27
    Pension costs 28

Capitalisation of interest	29
Extraordinary items	29
Dividends	30

5 Group accounting — 31
Introduction — 31
The Seventh Directive — 31
The group — 33
Valuation rules for consolidation — 35
Consolidation techniques — 36
Minority interests — 37
Associates and joint ventures — 37
Translation — 38
    Transactions — 38
    Translation of foreign financial statements — 39
Segmental reporting — 40

6 Current and future developments — 41

Appendices

I Formats — 43
  1 UK, balance sheet, format 1 (vertical) — 44
  2 UK, profit and loss account, format 1 — 45
  3 UK, profit and loss account, format 2 — 46
  4 Belgium, balance sheet — 47
  5 Belgium, profit and loss account (two-sided) — 48
  6 Italy, balance sheet — 49
  7 Italy, profit and loss account — 50
  8 Spain, balance sheet — 52
  9 Spain, profit and loss account — 53

II Glossary — 55

Chapter 1

Setting the scene

The background to European accounting

1.1 Accounting has developed over thousands of years, and Europe has played a major rôle. Accounting records have survived from classical Greece and Rome, but it is fairly clear that double-entry bookkeeping was invented in the northern Italian city states in the thirteenth century. It was several centuries before it became common practice in the other three countries examined in this book. Later, the British pioneered the ideas of the accountancy profession and of compulsory publication and audit of financial statements. The Germans and French invented and developed ideas of uniform accounting. The Dutch have led the world in techniques of current value accounting.

1.2 Over the centuries, various factors have shaped accounting differently throughout Europe. As a result, European differences in financial reporting are major, deep-seated and long-lasting. The factors that cause differences include the legal system, users of statements, the tax system and the profession. These are discussed briefly in turn below.

1.3 There are two major legal systems in the Western developed world: Roman (generally codified) legal systems and the English common law system. The former operate throughout most of continental Europe and usually involve extensive prescription from government. By contrast, common law countries tend to survive on limited amounts of government-set rules. In accounting, this tends to mean that Roman countries (such as Belgium, Italy and Spain) have many rules in law, particularly in a commercial or civil code. By contrast, the UK has traditionally relied upon professional judgement, although this has increasingly been written down as accounting standards.

1.4 In Belgium and Spain, much of the detail of government-controlled rules may be found in accounting plans, which are enforced by law. In Belgium, a government appointed commission issues guidelines on

Setting the scene

interpretation of laws and decrees. In Italy, from the 1970s onwards there has been an attempt to move, for listed companies, towards standards that are somewhat like Anglo-American accounting standards.

1.5 The second influential factor is the nature of corporate owners and financiers, and hence users of financial statements. In much of continental Europe, corporate finance has traditionally come from banks, governments or family members. This means that the major financiers are board members and can obtain up-to-date detailed information as directors. Consequently, there has traditionally been no great demand for publication of financial reports or for external audit. The small size of the profession in Belgium and Spain is evidence of this, as is the small number of listed companies (see Tables 1 and 2). In Italy, the large size of the professional bodies (as shown in Table 1) is misleading because a very large proportion of the members are not involved in external audit. It should be noted that Belgium and Italy do not feature in Table 2, because they have fewer than 250 domestic listed companies (Belgium, 143; Italy, 217). Furthermore, even those few listed companies that exist in continental Europe are extensively held by the banks, governments or families, thus reducing the pressure for public accountability and audit. By contrast, in the UK there is a long history of corporate financing from large numbers of 'outsiders' who demand audited published information. Consequently, there are many listed companies and many auditors.

1.6 The third factor is the tax system. Simply put, taxation rules influence many of the details of normal continental European accounting, such as the valuation of assets, the measurement of depreciation and the calculation of bad debt and other provisions. For most purposes, the figures in the financial accounts should be the same as those in the tax accounts. This is the traditional principle in Belgium, Italy and Spain, but not in the UK, where taxation rules are different from accounting rules for several matters, sometimes giving rise to substantial amounts of deferred tax. In Spain particularly, moves have been made away from the traditional influence.

1.7 Fourthly, the accountancy profession is old and strong in the UK where it plays a major part in setting the standards for accounting and for auditing. Much of the detail of UK rules is to be found in Statements of Standard Accounting Practice (SSAPs) and, from 1990, Financial Reporting Standards (FRSs) which are set by an independent committee. These are recognised in law but are not part of the law. They are binding on auditors, and directors must disclose non-compliance. In Belgium, Italy and Spain, the profession is newer, smaller and weaker. Governments or government-run committees control most of the rules of accounting and auditing. However, in Italy, professionally set accounting principles *(principi contabili)* are of some relevance to listed companies. This is because the Stock Exchange regulatory body (CONSOB) recommends that listed companies should follow these in the absence of other rules. Other Italian entities, such as banks and government-controlled companies are subject to similar rules.

Setting the scene

Table 1
Some professional bodies

Country	Body	Founded*	Size (000s)
UK and Ireland	Institute of Chartered Accountants in England and Wales	1880 (1870)	107
	Association of Chartered Certified Accountants	1939 (1891)	47
	Institute of Chartered Accountants of Scotland	1951 (1854)	13
	Institute of Chartered Accountants in Ireland	1888	9
Belgium	Institut des Reviseurs d'Enterprises (Instituut der Bedrijfsrevisoren)	1953	1
Italy	Consiglio Nazionale dei Dottori Commercialisti	1924	36
	Collegio dei Ragionieri e Periti Commerciali	1906	33
Spain	Instituto de Censores Jurados de Cuentas de España	1945	6
	Registro de Economistas Auditores	1982	4
Netherlands	Nederlands Instituut van Registeraccountants	1895	9
France	Ordre des Experts Comptables et des Comptables Agréés	1945 (1881)	13
Germany	Institut der Wirtschaftsprüfer	1932	7
United States	American Institute of Certified Public Accountants	1887	315
Japan	Japanese Institute of Certified Public Accountants	1948	13

* Date of founding of earliest predecessor is in brackets.

Table 2
Stock exchanges with over 250 domestic listed companies*

Europe:	Germany	437
	London	1,701
	Madrid	361
	Paris	710
	Switzerland	216
Americas:	NASDAQ	4,760
	New York	2,428
	Toronto	1,196
Asia, Africa:	Australian	1,129
	Hong Kong	518
	Johannesburg	614
	Tokyo	1,714

*Note: There are also a number of non-domestic companies listed on these exchanges. The above numbers exclude investment funds.

Source: London Stock Exchange *Fact Book*, 1996, p49.

EU harmonisation

1.8 The Commission of the European Communities has been the driving force behind the efforts to reduce the differences in accounting and auditing in the EU member states. The main mechanisms for this are Directives, which are drafted by the Commission, adopted by the Council of Ministers and implemented by the Parliaments of the member states. Table 3 shows a list of Directives on company law, of which the Fourth and Seventh are of greatest importance for financial reporting. The Fourth concerns formats of financial statements, accounting principles, and requirements for disclosure, publication and audit. It was brought into force for the four countries considered here as follows:

Setting the scene

UK	Companies Act 1981 (now included in the 1985 Act)
Belgium	Accounting Law of 17 July 1975 (amended slightly by later Royal Decrees)
Italy	Law of 9 April 1991
Spain	Law 19 of 25 July 1989

1.9 The Seventh Directive concerns consolidated accounts. Whereas the Fourth Directive was largely based on German law, the Seventh was approximately based on British practice. It was implemented by the Companies Act 1989 in the UK, and in Italy and Spain by the same law that implemented the Fourth Directive. In Belgium, the Seventh Directive was implemented by a Royal Decree of March 1990, (applied to listed companies by a Royal Decree of November 1991). The details of these Directives are covered under various headings in the following chapters.

Table 3

Directives relevant to corporate accounting

Directives on Company Law	Draft Dates	Date Adopted	Purpose
First	1964	1968	Ultra vires rules
Second	1970, 1972	1976	Separation of public companies, minimum capital, distributions
Third	1970, 1973 1975	1978	Mergers
Fourth	1971, 1974	1978	Formats and rules of accounting
Fifth	1972, 1983	–	Structure and audit of public companies
Sixth	1975, 1978	1982	De-mergers
Seventh	1976, 1978	1983	Consolidated accounting
Eighth	1978, 1979	1984	Qualifications and work of auditors
Ninth	–	–	Links between public company groups
Tenth	1985	–	International mergers of public companies
Eleventh	1986	1989	Disclosures relating to branches
Twelfth	1988	1989	Single member companies
Thirteenth	1989	–	Takeovers
Vredeling	1980, 1983	–	Employee information and consultation

Chapter 2

Companies, publication, audit and formats

Companies

2.1 In each of our four countries there are both public and private companies (names shown below). In each case, only public companies are allowed to create a market in their securities, although most public companies are not listed on stock exchanges. Other than in the UK, there are also limited partnerships with shares (for example, in Italy, Società in Accomandita per Azioni (SAPA)). These are less common.

UK	B
Private Limited Company (Ltd)	Besloten Vennootschap met
Public Limited Company (PLC)	Beperkte Aansprakelijkheid
	(BVBA) or Société à
	Responsabilité Limitée (Sarl)
	Naamloze Vennootschap (NV) or Société
	Anonyme (SA)
I	S
Società a Responsabilità Limitata (Srl)	Sociedad de Responsabilidad Limitada (SRL)
Società per Azioni (SpA)	Sociedad Anónima (SA)

The minimum capital requirements for companies are:

UK	–	PLCs	–	£50,000
Belgium	–	NV/SA	–	BF 2.5m
		BVBA/Sarl	–	BF 0.75m
Italy	–	SpA	–	Lit 200m
		SRL	–	Lit 20m
Spain	–	SA	–	Pts 10m
		SRL	–	Pts 0.5m

2.2 In many areas, the rules for banks and insurance companies are different, and this book does not specifically cover such companies

2.3 The Fourth Directive's rules allow various exemptions for private companies depending on their size. Approximately speaking, the size category of a company is determined by whether it falls below two of the three size limits shown below.

For small companies:

	UK	B*
Turnover:	£2.8 million	BF 200 million
Balance sheet total:	£1.4 million	BF 100 million
Employees:	50	50
	I	S
Turnover:	Lit 9.5 bn	Pts 790 million
Balance sheet total:	Lit 4.7 bn	Pts 395 million
Employees:	50	50

* Companies with a works council (certainly those with over 100 employees) automatically fall outside this category.

For medium-sized companies:

	UK	B
Turnover:	£11.2 million	Not relevant
Balance sheet total:	£5.6 million	
Employees:	250	
	I	S
Turnover:	Not relevant	Pts 3160 million
Balance sheet total:		Pts 1580 million
Employees:		250

Publication and audit

2.4 The exemptions from publication and audit are as follows for small companies:

UK	B
Exemption from publication of profit and loss account, directors' report and many notes; and balance sheet may be abbreviated. Companies with a turnover and balance sheet total below £350,000 and £1.4m respectively do not generally require to be audited. These exemptions depend on the company being private.	Abbreviated formats for financial statements Exempt from audit, except when part of a group that publishes consolidated financial statements.
I	S
Abbreviated balance sheet and notes can be published.	Abbreviated formats for financial statements. Exempt from audit.

For medium sized companies:

UK	B
Abbreviated profit and loss account (for publication purposes only).	Not relevant.
I	S
Not relevant.	Abbreviated profit and loss account.

2.5 A curiosity relating only to the UK is that the parent company's profit and loss account does not need to be drawn up or published in cases where group accounts are produced. The parent's balance sheet must be published, and is normally included in the group accounts.

2.6 'Publication' may mean slightly different things in different countries. In the UK, Spain and Italy, it means depositing financial statements with the Registrar of Companies (or equivalent). In Belgium, from 1991, annual accounts have to be deposited at the National Bank of Belgium. For listed companies in Belgium, an extract must be published in a newspaper.

2.7 In Italy, until 1993, only listed companies, government-owned companies, some banks and others were required to have a full independent expert audit. (Even now, unqualified auditors who were acting before the change in rules can continue.) All companies continue to have audit by *sindaci*, who might be compared to internal auditors. These 'statutory auditors' are appointed by the shareholders, but do not carry out a full audit in the Anglo-Saxon sense.

2.8 Filing deadlines are somewhat different in the four countries. The limits below are from the balance sheet date:

UK	B
Private companies: 10 months. Public companies: 7 months.	Six months, or one month after the AGM.
I	S
Normally 5 months, but can be extended to 7.	One month after approval by AGM, which must be within 6 months from the balance sheet date.

2.9 Certain types of disclosure are required in some countries but not in others. Some of these disclosures are considered here:

(i) Statements of cash flows or fund flows	
UK	B
Cash flow statements required by FRS 1. Small private companies and greater that 90 per cent owned subsidiaries are exempted.	Provision of flow statements is the majority practice by large listed companies, but not required and not uniform.
I	S
Flow statements recommended by Standard 12. All government-controlled companies publish these.	Funds flow statements required by law. Details in accounting plan.
(ii) Earnings per share	
UK	B
Required to be disclosed by SSAP 3 for listed companies.	Majority practice by large listed companies to publish 'dividends per share' but not required.

I Not required. A few listed companies publish these.	S Not required, and uncommon.
(iii) Interim reports	
UK Half-yearly (unaudited) summary reports required by the Listing Requirements of the London Stock Exchange.	B Half-yearly reports required for listed companies.
I Half-yearly reports required by CONSOB for listed companies. CONSOB recommends audit or audit review.	S Unaudited quarterly financial statements required by the Stock Exchange.

Other general accounting features

Accounting for changing prices

2.10 In none of our four countries are there presently requirements for reporting on a price-adjusted basis. A few companies in the UK volunteer to do this.

Accounting policy changes

2.11 In the UK, material accounting policy changes must be disclosed and treated as prior period adjustments. In the other countries, the effects of changes are absorbed in the year of change, with disclosure and justification for any changes.

Prior period adjustments

2.12 In the UK, prior period adjustments are made (according to FRS 3) for corrections of fundamental errors or after changes in accounting policies. In Belgium, Italy and Spain, this practice is not accepted. All adjustments must go through the year's profit and loss account. Except in Spain, where material items must be disclosed and explained, prior period adjustments need not be separately disclosed, although good practice requires this.

Post balance sheet events

2.13 In the UK, according to SSAP 17, material post balance sheet events can be 'adjusting' (when the balance sheet is adjusted because the events give better information on matters that already existed at the balance sheet date, for example, facts relating to debtors) or 'non-adjusting' (when note information is to be given because the events relate to matters that did not exist at the balance sheet date, for example, a destructive fire). Practice in Belgium and Spain is to recognise losses from 'adjusting' events, but not gains. In Italy, listed company practice is much as in the UK; the law requires disclosure, and *principi contabili* contain similar recommendations to the UK's.

Related party transactions

2.14 In all the countries, intra-group balances are disclosed separately in individual company accounts. The UK's FRS 8 requires extensive disclosures of transactions with a wide range of related parties. In the other countries, there are no specific requirements for disclosures, outside the rules relating to directors.

Formats

2.15 There were two balance sheet formats and four profit and loss account formats in the Fourth Directive. The profit and loss formats are vertical and two-sided forms of the 'gross profit' concept or the 'total output' concept (see Appendix I for the formats).

	UK	B
Balance sheet:	Both allowed. Vertical normal.	Two-sided only.
Profit & loss:	All allowed. Vertical normal. 'Gross profit' most usual.	Vertical and two-sided versions of the 'total output' format. For group accounts, 'gross profit' is also allowed.
	I	S
Balance sheet:	Two-sided.	Two-sided only.
Profit & loss:	Vertical form of the 'total output' format.	Two-sided form of the 'total output' format.

2.16 The UK's 'statement of total recognised gains and losses' is not found in the other three countries.

Chapter 3

Valuation of assets

Principles of valuation

3.1 Under the Fourth Directive, there is a three-tier hierarchy of principles:

- There is the requirement that directors shall ensure that the annual accounts give a 'true and fair view' (UK), *getrouw beeld* or *image fidèle* (B), *in modo veritiero e corretto* (I) and *imagen fiel* (E). In all countries, this is an overriding requirement and should lead, where necessary, to extra disclosures or even to departures from the second and third tier of principles.

  However, it is clear that the degree to which the judgement of truth and fairness rests with individual accountants varies internationally. In the UK, where there is a tradition of professional judgement, originally uncluttered by written rules, the need for truth and fairness is supposed to be not only in the minds of legislators and standard setters but also a constant reference point for finance directors and auditors when preparing annual accounts.

  In Belgium, Italy and Spain, the 'true and fair' requirement only arrived recently. It is still generally assumed by accountants and auditors that compliance with detailed rules will ensure truth and fairness.

- The second tier of principles is also now common to all countries that have implemented the Fourth Directive. The principles are:

  - The accounts are to be prepared on the basis that the company is a going concern; if it is not, that fact should be disclosed.

  - The accruals or matching concept.

  - Conservatism or prudence, including only taking realised profits.

Valuation of assets

- Consistency of policies from year to year.

- Valuation of items individually before aggregation.

Despite international uniformity of these principles, there is still plenty of scope for differences in interpretation, especially because the principles can be contradictory. For example, in Italy, there is a long tradition of greater conservatism than in the UK. Examples of extra conservatism are discussed under the topic headings later in this chapter. Also, most countries have more accounting principles than those specified by the Directive.

- The third tier of principles are detailed valuation rules. This tier, and the second tier, were missing from the law of the UK until 1981, but were present in detail in Belgium and Italy. The best way of examining this third tier is to look at particular assets, as below.

Tangible fixed assets

3.2 The valuation of fixed assets is an area where there is much variety and where the Fourth Directive allows many options to member states or companies. Although the basic rules require assets to be valued at purchase price or production cost, member states such as the UK and the Netherlands insisted that alternatives must be allowed. The main achievement of the Directive has been to ensure that, where a company departs from strict historical cost, details must be given of the valuation methods used and what the historical cost figures would have been. This is especially relevant for large companies in the UK who tend to make use of the 'alternative valuation rules'.

3.3 The data below summarises the practice in the four countries:

UK	B
Majority use of historical cost, except that many large companies revalue assets from time to time to market values, particularly for land and buildings. It is also possible to revalue every year, and to use replacement costs for some or all assets. Investment properties must be revalued annually. Finance leases are capitalised.	Historical cost, except that tangible fixed assets may be increased if their value has clearly and permanently risen. Leases are capitalisable under conditions similar to Anglo-American rules. The tax treatment follows the accounting treatment.
I	S
Historical cost, except that revaluations in 1975, 1983, 1990 and 1991 were allowed or required. Leases are not capitalised.	Historical cost, but revaluations have been allowed (most recently in 1996). Finance leases are accounted for as intangibles (see below).

3.4 Government grants for fixed assets are treated in two main ways in the UK: by treating the grant as a deferred credit amortised over the life of the asset, or by deducting the grant from the cost of the asset. Both methods would give the same profit figures. SSAP 4 suggests that the latter method is illegal under the Companies Act 1985.

3.5 In Italy, government grants are normally shown as part of 'other reserves' and are not credited to profit and loss. In Belgium, such grants are treated as 'investment reserves'; additions since 1993 are shown net of deferred tax, which is separately recorded as a liability. In Spain they appear as deferred credits, shown between shareholders' funds and liabilities. In Belgium and Spain, the grants are taken to profit and loss over the life of the asset.

Intangibles

3.6 The Fourth Directive allows companies to record intangibles as assets at their purchase cost, although member states may allow them to be recorded at current cost (the UK does so). In addition, member states may allow companies to capitalise formation expenses and research and development. Formation expenses must not be capitalised in the UK, but may be capitalised and written off over up to five years in the other three countries. Development expenditure can be capitalised under certain

Valuation of assets

conditions and written off over its useful economic life in the UK and Belgium. In Italy and Spain, both research and development may be capitalised if they have future worth; and then they must be amortised over a period of up to five years. In Italy various 'deferred costs', such as advertising expenditures, may be capitalised.

3.7 In Spain, rights over assets being acquired under finance leases are now capitalised as intangible assets, rather than as tangible assets as in the UK and several other countries. They are depreciated in the same way as for tangible fixed assets. Brand names, where purchased individually or as part of a business combination, may be separately identified and valued in all four countries. In the UK, there has been controversy because some companies have recently gone further than this by putting a balance sheet value (technically, a current cost) on created or formerly purchased brands. This latter is not the practice in the other three countries.

3.8 Goodwill is discussed in chapter 5.

Investments

3.9 Long-term investments are generally held at cost, with dividends recorded as income. However, in Spain, even long-term investments are reduced to market value if it is lower. By contrast, long-term investments can be revalued upwards in Belgium and the UK. In all our four countries, the equity method is only used in group accounts: for associates and unconsolidated subsidiaries. In Italy, investments in subsidiaries or associates can be held using the equity method in individual company accounts. In practice, because of tax effects, cost generally remains the practice.

3.10 Current asset investments are generally held at the lower of cost and net realisable value. However, in the UK, it is increasingly common for current asset marketable securities to be shown at current value, with the implied gains or losses taken to profit and loss account. This is called 'marking to market' and was proposed by ED 55 of 1990. In other countries, current asset investments are held at the lower of cost and market.

Stocks

3.11 The Fourth Directive requires the use of prudence, which entails the well established valuation practice of the 'lower of cost and market'. For determining 'cost' the Directive permits member states to allow the use of

FIFO, LIFO, weighted average or similar method, where individual valuation is not appropriate. Any value adjustments solely for tax purposes must be disclosed.

3.12 These rules clearly allow scope for international differences; and the Directive does not cover the topic of overheads. The practices of the four countries may be summarised as follows:

UK	B
FIFO is the usual basis. SSAP 9 states that the use of LIFO would not usually be 'fair' (and case law prohibits its use for tax purposes). Consequently, LIFO is very rare. 'Market' is taken to mean net realisable value. Production overheads are included in cost, but administrative and selling overheads are not to be included. Long-term contracts are valued on the percentage-of-completion basis, with profit capable of being included before completion. The asset thereby recorded representing work carried out to date less payments on account is shown as a debtor (amount recoverable on contracts) rather than as an addition to stock.	Stocks are valued at the lower of cost and net realisable value. Individual valuation, weighted average, LIFO or FIFO are allowed. Overheads may be included. Long-term contracts may be valued by percentage-of-completion or completed contract, and both are used.
I	**S**
Stocks may be valued at FIFO, weighted average, or LIFO, and the latter is often used for tax reasons. 'Market' means net realisable value. Production overheads are included. The completed contract method is used for long-term contracts by many companies. Others use the percentage-of completion method with a tax deductible reserve.	Stocks are valued at the lower of cost or market. The latter can mean net realisable value or replacement cost. Production overheads are included. Where individual valuation is not appropriate, weighted average is preferred. However, FIFO and LIFO are allowed. The treatment of long-term contracts is not specified, although most companies use the completed contract method, for tax reasons.

Debtors and creditors

3.13 As a result of prudence, debtors are valued in most countries at expected future receipts rather than at legal obligations outstanding. That is, provisions for specific doubtful debts are deducted from debtors and charged as an expense. In Italy and Spain, even general provisions within specific limits on debts (overdue debts, in Spain) are tax-deductible and therefore subject to the tendency of management to raise them above what would be commercially realistic, within the overall control of tax rules.

3.14 The Fourth Directive requires separate disclosure of any amounts included under debtors (and therefore included in 'current' assets) that are not expected to be received within one year from the balance sheet date.

3.15 In all four countries, a current liability is one due within one year; and this is in accordance with the Fourth Directive. In Spain, the dividing line between current and non-current was 18 months, until the implementation of the Fourth Directive for 1990 year ends.

3.16 In the UK, foreign currency debtors and creditors are translated at year-end rates, with differences being taken to the profit and loss account. In Spain, too, year-end rates are used, but translation differences are divided into categories by maturity of the balances and convertibility of the currencies; then the net total on each category is calculated, and taken to income if a loss, or deferred if a gain. In Italy, more than one method is possible. However, usually the translation rate at the date of the transaction is used. If the year-end rate would give a worse value, a double entry will be recorded to take a loss and to record a balancing provision for foreign exchange risks. In Belgium, translation at year-end rates is allowed but not the recommended practice, as unrealised exchange gains on the net position in foreign currencies are normally deferred until realisation.

Contingencies

3.17 In the UK, according to SSAP 18, probable contingent losses should be accounted for as liabilities. Probable contingent gains and all reasonably possible contingent gains or losses should be disclosed in the notes. In Belgium, Italy and Spain, practice for contingent losses is similar to this, with foreseeable losses being accounted for. In Italy disclosure (as memorandum accounts) of certain contingencies (for example, guarantees) not accounted for is made below the balance on the liabilities side of the

Reserves and provisions

3.18 The distinction between reserves and provisions is broadly similar throughout the four countries, but the occasions on which provisions are seen as appropriate differs internationally. This can have a spectacular effect on total liabilities, which explains the inclusion of this topic in this chapter. Of course, there is an equal effect on profits.

3.19 In the UK, at least, provisions are estimates of losses or expenses which relate to events before the balance sheet date. They are liabilities and are created by a charge against profit. Reserves are an allocation of profit once it has been calculated. The setting up of one reserve merely involves the diminution of another.

3.20 In Belgium, Italy and Spain, the concept of prudence requires (and the Fourth Directive allows) that specific provisions be set up for uncertain liabilities even if there are no obligations at the balance sheet date. This will sometimes lead to greater provisions and more flexibility relating to the provisions and their reversal.

3.21 An example of a *reserve* found in all four countries is the revaluation reserve relating to previous asset revaluations. Another reserve found in Belgium, Italy and Spain is the legal reserve, which comprises appropriations from profit to this undistributable reserve. The annual appropriations must be 5 per cent of profit (10 per cent in Spain) until the reserve reaches 20 per cent of issued share capital (10 per cent for Belgium). This reserve is designed to protect creditors.

3.22 In Belgium, certain profits are exempted from taxation if they are kept as 'tax free reserves'. Since 1993, additions to such reserves must be shown net of deferred tax, with the latter shown as a liability.

Chapter 4

Measurement of profit

Principles of measurement

4.1 The three levels of principles referred to in chapter 3 also apply to profit measurement, that is:

- The requirement to give a true and fair view.

- The principles of going concern, accruals, prudence, consistency and individual valuation.

- Detailed valuation rules.

4.2 Because of the direct linkage between asset valuation and profit measures, the other facts of chapter three are also relevant here. For example, a conservative valuation of fixed assets or stocks will lead to a lower profit figure.

4.3 The Fourth Directive has no detailed instructions that relate purely to profit calculation, except that turnover figures should be shown net of returns, rebates, VAT and other taxes linked to turnover. There are, of course, instructions about the disclosure and location of certain figures, which are discussed in various places in this book.

4.4 Some topics which have a major effect on profit measurement are discussed in this chapter.

Depreciation

4.5 The Fourth Directive requires fixed assets with limited useful lives to be depreciated systematically over these lives. Further value adjustments are required where falls in value are expected to be permanent.

4.6 It is useful to divide the countries in two as far as depreciation rules are concerned:

Source of rules

UK

The driving force behind the calculation of depreciation charges is professionally-set accounting standards. These involve the estimation of asset lives and scrap values. In theory, the manner of wearing out of the asset should also be considered, although in practice the straight-line method is dominant, because it is simple. Depreciation for *tax* purposes is a different matter in the UK, as capital allowances (that is, tax depreciation) are a quite separate scheme. Consequently, depreciation is a source of the timing differences which create deferred tax.

Belgium, Italy and Spain

Depreciation for financial reporting purposes is heavily influenced by tax rules. So, for example, it is not necessary in Belgium (nor, in practice, for individual companies in Italy) to estimate an asset's life or scrap value, because accounting depreciation is based on the tax tables for the particular asset in its particular location. Often the asset lives implied by the tax depreciation rates are broadly in line with commercial reality. However, accelerated tax depreciation is fairly common for certain assets or certain areas. At the extreme, this could lead to new assets being immediately written down to zero for tax and, therefore, for accounting. However, best practice is to show the effects of accelerated depreciation in notes and in Italy to comment on it in the directors' report. In Spain, until the reform which became effective in 1990, depreciation was based solely on fiscal criteria, but must now be based on useful lives. However, in practice, fiscally allowable rates generally continue to be used, except that accelerated depreciation is only permissible in the accounts where the lives of the assets warrant it.

Measurement of profit

Revaluation

UK

Where fixed assets have been revalued upwards, depreciation charges are based on the revalued amounts and, consequently, will rise.

(Investment and Commercial Properties:
One peculiar feature of UK practice is the lack of depreciation of investment properties, which is the required treatment under SSAP 19 in order to give a true and fair view. This runs counter to the Directive's detailed instructions and is not found in other EU countries. Furthermore, the fairly widespread UK practice of not depreciating some commercial properties, because they have been fully maintained is not followed elsewhere.)

Italy and Spain

Revaluation has occurred in accordance with tax and other regulations, as mentioned in chapter three. Depreciation under these circumstances is also controlled by tax rules, and generally rises with the assets.

Belgium

Where fixed assets have been revalued, depreciation charges follow this (though not for tax purposes).

Deferred tax

4.7 Deferred tax arises as a result of the recognition of the effect of reversible timing differences between the treatment of an item as an expense or revenue for accounting purposes and its treatment for tax purposes. Consequently, where accounting and tax are closely related (see chapter 1), significant amounts of deferred tax will not arise. For our four countries, this means that deferred tax has been a major issue in the UK, but traditionally unimportant in Belgium, Italy and Spain.

4.8 In more detail, in the UK, deferred tax is accounted for on a partial allocation basis, that is, to the extent that it is probable that a liability or an asset will crystallise. The 'liability method' is used in all four countries, in that changes in corporation tax rates are taken into account. The UK rules are to be found in SSAP 15.

4.9 In Belgium and Spain, the importance of deferred tax has increased with the implementation of the Directives. With the introduction of the legislation on consolidated accounts in Belgium in 1990, companies have to restate to economic or comparable valuation rules and this can give rise to deferred taxes in the consolidated accounts (either accounted for or disclosed in the notes). Deferred tax may also arise where group accounting rules are different from those used by individual companies in the group. Also, in Belgium for 1993 onwards, capital subsidies, which used to be accounted for fully as part of reserves, must now have the deferred tax element recorded as a liability. In addition, deferred tax must be recognised on temporarily tax exempted realised gains on fixed assets. In Spain, also, since 1990 there can be differences between tax and accounting figures. For example, accelerated tax depreciation (of up to 100 per cent in some areas of Spain) should not now be recorded in the accounts, but deferred tax should be accounted for.

4.10 In Italy, deferred tax would not normally arise in the individual company accounts; nor in group accounts, except for such amounts carried through to group accounts from foreign subsidiaries, and in Italy for deferred taxes on the sale of fixed assets. However, for Italian group accounts, deferred tax is provided for timing differences such as accelerated depreciation or some provisions.

Pension costs

4.11 The subject of pension costs is very complex and will not be dealt with in detail here. However, some major points of international difference should be noted. In the UK, SSAP 24 requires an accruals basis to be used, such that the pension expenses recorded in any year's profit and loss account results from an allocation of the eventual cost of an employee's pension over his/her service period. All pension commitments must be provided for on this basis. By contrast, the rules in Belgium do not require full provision, and it is sufficient to disclose these amounts as contingent liabilities. In such cases, the charge in the profit and loss account would be made on a cash basis. For example, in Belgium, the pension expense is recorded as the amount paid into the external pension fund in the year, including any large single payments made to attract tax reliefs.

4.12 The situation in Spain is similar to that for the UK, except that provisions were generally not made until 1990. From that date, pension costs charged in any year have been those relating to the year *plus*, transitionally, a minimum of 1/15th of unprovided past service costs in respect of active employees and 1/7th for retired employees. A ruling by the regulatory body appears to permit all companies to charge those amounts against reserves each year, instead of against profits. There are no rules with respect to the methods of calculation, except that an actuarially approved method must be used.

4.13 In Italy, pensions are paid by the state, partly from payments made by the company. Thus, no provisions are necessary. However, when employees leave a company, for whatever reason, severance pay must be made, and this is accrued in the accounts.

Capitalisation of interest

4.14 Capitalisation of interest on construction projects is legal in the UK under the Companies Act 1985. It is the practice of some companies. In Spain, capitalisation is allowed but somewhat unusual, although it is found in the construction industry. It is fairly common in Belgium and Italy for long-term projects.

Extraordinary items

4.15 The definition of extraordinary items varies from country to country. Extraordinary items are shown separately in all countries. The treatments are as follows:

UK	B
Items are extraordinary if they are material, outside the ordinary activities of the business, and not expected to recur. FRS 3's definition of 'ordinary' is so wide that little or nothing would be extraordinary. Exceptional items are abnormal in size or incidence. Some of these must be shown on the face of the profit and loss account and others in the notes.	Items are extraordinary if they do not relate to the ordinary activities of the business. This includes several specific items, for example, exceptional gains and losses on disposal of fixed assets, and write-offs of investments.

I	S
Extraordinaries are vaguely defined in line with the Fourth Directive (ie, outside ordinary activities) so practice varies.	The standard format of accounts contains a specific caption for extraordinary items, although the permissible items for inclusion are much wider than in the UK and include prior year charges, gains or losses on the sale of fixed assets and dealings in own shares. Items need not be individually significant for aggregation in this caption.

Dividends

4.16 In the UK and Belgium, proposed dividends are accrued in the financial statements even when they still await shareholder approval. They are shown as appropriations and current liabilities. In Italy and Spain, only paid (or declared) dividends are accounted for. This means that British and Belgian companies show lower retained profits and higher liabilities than in the other countries, on this particular point.

Chapter 5

Group accounting

Introduction

5.1 The general practice and most of the details of consolidation are American inventions of the past 100 years. UK practices have gradually arrived from across the Atlantic. The easiest description of UK practices is to say that they are largely those of the US, but with more flexibility and a decade's time lag.

5.2 In stark contrast, consolidation has been a rarity in much of continental Europe. This is partly due to the dominance of tax authorities and banks, who are less interested in consolidated accounts than parent company shareholders are. In Belgium, Italy and Spain, consolidation was a rarity at least until the 1980s. In Italy, listed groups (those controlled by CONSOB) have been required to prepare consolidated accounts since the late 1970s. In Belgium and Spain, consolidation is largely a result of the implementation of the Seventh Directive.

5.3 Not only has the extent of use of consolidation varied in Europe, but also the techniques employed. In nearly every area of consolidation practice, European differences can be found: the definition of subsidiaries and of associates; the calculation of and writing-off of goodwill; the treatment of joint ventures and of unincorporated subsidiaries; and so on.

5.4 Particularly for large listed companies, whose shareholders and lenders may be of several nationalities, the existence of differences creates such problems that the European Commission has intervened to try to harmonise the rules. Clearly, this is having a major effect on our four countries, and a consideration of harmonisation of group accounting follows.

The Seventh Directive

5.5 As shown in chapter one, the Seventh Directive was adopted by the Council of Ministers in 1983. It was designed to be enacted by 1 January

Group accounting

1988 and to be applied to accounts for years beginning on or after 1 January 1990. The only EU members to have managed this schedule were France and Germany, although the UK, the Netherlands, Greece and Luxembourg achieved the latter target. Spain and Portugal were allowed to delay implementation, although both implemented laws with effect for financial years beginning on or after 1 January 1991.

5.6 In general terms, the Directive requires the following:

- Parents must produce group accounts in the form of consolidation.

- Domestic and foreign subsidiaries must be included, and this is irrespective of legal form of the subsidiary.

- The group accounts must give a true and fair view.

- The formats of the Fourth Directive must be adopted, and adapted for the consolidated accounts.

- Associates must be accounted for in group accounts by using the equity method of 'one-line consolidation'.

5.7 Other matters are addressed by the Directive but with variations allowed, as explained in the following sections. Such matters include the calculation and treatment of goodwill; the use of merger accounting and proportional consolidation; the exclusion of certain subsidiaries; the exemption for parents that are themselves subsidiaries; the exemption for groups that are 'small'.

5.8 Some facts relating to implementation are shown opposite:

UK	B
Implementation in Companies Act 1989. In force for accounting periods beginning on or after 23.12.1989.	Implemented by the Royal Decree of 6 March 1990. In force for years beginning on or after 1.1.1991.
I	S
Implementation by law of 9 April 1991. In force for 1994 year ends.	Implementation by Law 19 of 25 July 1989. In force for years beginning on or after 1.1.1991.

The group

5.9 Before the Seventh Directive there was great European variety in the definitions of a subsidiary. The British view tended towards the auditable notions of ownership of shares or control of board appointments. Some continental countries based their view on the concept of unified control; this is a sounder philosophical basis for defining a group for consolidation, but is vaguer. The Directive contains several conditions, drawn from different countries, that will mean that a parent-subsidiary relationship exists.

5.10 The emergence of the phenomenon of controlled non-subsidiaries made it clearer in the UK that the former definitions were too easily defeated by those wishing to leave companies out of consolidation. The Companies Act 1989 takes advantage of the wide-ranging definitions in the Directive. Common to all four countries are the following situations proving the existence of a parent-subsidiary relationship:

- A majority hold of voting rights.

- The right to appoint or remove directors holding a majority of votes on the board (the parent must be a member).

- The right to exercise a dominant influence by a control contract or by provisions in the memorandum or articles.

- Control with the agreement of other shareholders (the parent must be a member).

5.11 Member states may also implement the following two further definitions:

- Where a majority of the board has in practice been appointed using the parent's voting rights (implemented in Belgium and Spain).

- Where the parent holds a participating interest and exercises dominant influence or manages itself and the subsidiary on a unified basis (implemented in the UK and Belgium).

5.12 The Directive also requires non-listed parents which are themselves wholly-owned subsidiaries to be exempted from preparing group accounts as long as the parent's parent is in the EU and prepares proper group accounts. The exemption also applies to 90 per cent-held parents where the minority shareholders approve. (Italy has implemented the Directive using a 95 per cent level, and Spain has an exemption down to the 50 per cent level.) These exemptions can be extended in various ways, as shown for the member states which have legislation:

UK	B
Exemption irrespective of the size of holdings, as long as there is no opposition by more than 50 per cent of the remaining shareholders or by holders of 5 per cent of the total shares.	Extension in cases where the ultimate parent is outside the EU and prepares 'equivalent' accounts. This latter term is not defined.
I	**S**
Exemption irrespective of the size of holdings, as long as there is no opposition from holders of 5 per cent of the total shares.	Extension down to a 50 per cent threshold.

5.13 Certain subsidiaries may be excluded from consolidation. This applies where subsidiaries: operate under severe long-term restrictions that substantially hinder control over assets or management; are immaterial (individually or when taken together); could only be included using information that would involve disproportionate expense or undue delay; or are held exclusively with a view to subsequent resale. In the UK, the first of these is a compulsory exclusion.

Group accounting

5.14 Also, subsidiaries *must* be excluded where they are so different from the rest of the group that their inclusion in the group accounts would not give a true and fair view. This provision is obviously very vague. In the UK one would expect it to be rarely used (according to ASC and ASB statements), but in other countries it is being interpreted more widely.

5.15 The Directive allows member states to exempt 'small' and 'medium-sized' unlisted groups from preparing consolidated accounts. The size criteria for exemption can be expressed in national laws either gross for the whole group or net of consolidation adjustments. For our countries, the exemption is allowed where groups fall below two of three thresholds:

	UK	B
Turnover:	£13.44m (gross); £11.2m (net)	BF 2000m
Balance sheet:	£6.72m (gross); £5.6m (net)	BF 1000m
Employees:	250	500
	I	S
Turnover	Lit 38bn (gross)	Pts 4800m
Balance Sheet:	Lit 19bn (gross)	Pts 2300m
Employees	250	500

5.16 In Belgium, apart from vertical consolidation (parent – subsidiaries), it is also necessary to make a horizontal consolidation (for consortiums) which mainly affect family-owned companies and groups that are under common control.

Valuation rules for consolidation

5.17 The Directive requires all member states to ensure that group accounts give a true and fair view and use the formats in the Fourth Directive (suitably amended for minority interests, etc). There must be elimination of intra-group debts and trading. Uniform accounting policies must be used within the group accounts, and this may entail adjusting assets and liabilities for the purposes of consolidation.

5.18 The Seventh Directive requires that, where tax-based values have been used in individual company accounts, these shall either be disclosed or corrected in the consolidated financial statements. The 'correction' route is possible, even in tax-driven countries, because the group accounts are not used for tax purposes. The consolidation adjustments designed to achieve the corrections give rise to the need to account for deferred tax. The 'disclosure' route means that assets will still be based on tax values in the group financial statements, but that there should be disclosures on this point in the notes.

5.19 The UK believes that this point is not relevant for it. In Belgium, Italy and Spain, the law allows both routes, but companies generally follow the 'disclosure' route.

5.20 Another relevant point here is that the Directive allows group accounts to use different valuation rules from those used by the parent. This is extensively used in France and Germany in order to allow large groups to use 'international' practice in group financial statements. Belgium and Italy also shows examples of this.

Consolidation techniques

5.21 The predominant method of consolidation in European practice and in the Seventh Directive is the acquisition (purchase) method, which is discussed in the rest of this section. However, the Directive allows the use of 'merger accounting', which is better known to many as the American 'pooling of interests' method. This method involves the use of book values for assets added to the group and nominal values for shares issued as consideration. No goodwill arises. Of the countries considered here, only the UK experiences the use of merger accounting. However, in Italy, Belgium and Spain, 'fusions' occur whereby mergers take place by transferring assets to a new company.

5.22 When using normal acquisition accounting, goodwill usually arises. Under the Directive, it must be calculated at the date of acquisition of a subsidiary (except for transitional cases). Goodwill is either to be calculated on the basis of fair values of net assets (as in the UK and Belgium) or initially on the basis of book values (as in Italy and Spain). In the latter method, the difference between the cost of the subsidiary and the book value of the net assets is then allocated to assets and liabilities on the basis of fair values; any remainder being goodwill. If there is positive goodwill, the two methods would appear to amount to the same thing. However, negative consolidation differences are less likely to arise under the latter method.

5.23 Goodwill may be either written off against reserves or amortised through the profit and loss account. Member states vary as follows:

UK	B
Companies may choose between deduction from reserves and amortisation over the useful economic life of the goodwill. The rules in law are extended in SSAP 22. Most UK companies have chosen immediate deduction from reserves to date, but new proposals will require capitalisation and amortisation over periods of up to 20 years. Longer periods will be allowed, but additional impairment tests will be required annually. Negative goodwill is shown as a reserve, although this is also likely to change under the new proposals.	Goodwill is capitalised and amortised over a period of up to 5 years. Longer periods are allowed, but justification is necessary. Negative goodwill is shown as a reserve.
I	S
Goodwill may either be written off against reserves immediately or be amortised over up to 5 years (or longer for special reasons). Negative goodwill should be shown as a liability or reserve, depending on its nature.	Goodwill is capitalised and amortised over up to 5 years (or up to 10 years with an explanation).

Minority interests

5.24 In Belgium, Spain and the UK, minority interests are treated as items intermediate between shareholders' funds and liabilities. By contrast, in Italy, minorities are seen as a form of ownership interest and are included in the total of shareholders' funds in a consolidated balance sheet.

Associates and joint ventures

5.25 Associates are those undertakings (not being subsidiaries) over which another company (or group) exercises significant influence. This state of affairs is presumed to exist where there is a holding of 20 per cent or more of the voting rights. In the case of Italy, the law presumes that a holding of 10 per cent or more of a listed company amounts to significant influence;

and, in Spain, the presumption begins at 3 per cent holdings of listed companies.

5.26 According to the Seventh Directive, associates must be treated in the consolidated financial statements by some version of the 'equity method'. At the date of acquisition, the associate is held either at its book value or at the group's proportion of its shareholder's funds. In either case, the goodwill (the difference between the method chosen and the other method) must be shown in the balance sheet or in the notes.

5.27 Each year, the group's proportion of profit is taken to the group profit and loss account and this amount (less dividends paid out of it) is added to the holding value of the associate.

5.28 The Directive allows member states to permit or require proportional consolidation, instead of equity accounting, for holdings in joint ventures. Under this method, the appropriate proportion of assets, liabilities, expenses and revenues is consolidated on a line-by-line basis. This method is allowed in all four countries, but in the UK for unincorporated joint ventures only. In Belgium and Spain it is found for unincorporated joint ventures in certain industries (for example, oil), and for 50/50 held companies.

Translation

5.29 The Directives do not include rules relating to foreign currency translation. Consequently, the variety of practice in the EU is even greater for this topic than for other matters connected with consolidation. In Spain, the law covers this issue. In the UK there is no law on the method of currency translation, but there is a standard (SSAP 20). In the other two countries, tax rules control the treatment in individual accounts, but there are no rules in group accounts.

Transactions

5.30 Description here will begin with the treatment of foreign currency items in an individual company's own accounts. In all the countries it is normal to translate assets into local currency once and for all. For example, consider a British company that bought on credit an Italian computer invoiced in lire. In the UK accounts, and assuming no forward purchasing or matching, this asset would normally be frozen into pounds sterling at the date of purchase.

5.31 The other matter is the resulting debtors or creditors in such cases. This point, and long-term monetary items in an individual company's accounts, has been considered in chapter three.

Translation of foreign financial statements

5.32 Companies in most countries, including our four, generally use the closing/current rate method for the translation of the accounts of foreign subsidiaries. This involves:

- Balance sheets translated at year-end rates.

- Profit and loss accounts translated at average rates for the year.

- Differences on translation put to reserves.

5.33 In the UK, SSAP 20 also allows, and many companies use, the closing rate for translating profit and loss accounts.

5.34 A further major point is the differential use of the temporal method, which used to be the standard US method in SFAS 8 from 1975 to 1981. It requires the use of exchange rates that are appropriate to the valuation basis of the item to be translated. For example, fixed assets (and depreciation charges on them) and stocks held at historical cost are translated at the appropriate historical rates; most profit and loss account items can normally be translated at average rates; cash and debtors are translated at year-end rates.

5.35 The temporal method (or the similar monetary/non-monetary method) is still used for the translation of the accounts of subsidiaries in hyper-inflationary countries under the present US rule, SFAS 52. In the UK, SSAP 20 calls for the use of this method for very closely held subsidiaries, as does SFAS 52 and the Spanish rules. However, in practice this is very rare in the UK. In Belgium, the temporal method is suggested as the preferred method, although the current rate method is more commonly used.

Segmental reporting

5.36 The Directives require turnover to be split by sector and market. Thus, this is required in our four countries. In the UK, the practice of most large companies goes further because SSAP 25 requires disclosure of turnover, pre-tax profit and net assets by both sector and market.

Chapter 6

Current and future developments

6.1 In chapter 1 there was an introductory discussion of the influences on the development of accounting in our four countries, including the effects of EU harmonisation. In the 1990s, the effects of the globalisation of capital markets have become clear. This has led to greater importance for world harmonisation of accounting and particularly for the work of the International Accounting Standards Committee (IASC).

6.2 The IASC was founded in 1973 by professional bodies from nine countries, including those of the UK (see Table 1 in chapter 1). Italy was a member of the Board of the IASC from 1983 to 1995. In 1997, the Board has 16 members. UK rules and practice have always been broadly compatible with IASs, but this is not the case for the other countries. Nevertheless, as noted earlier, many groups (particularly Italian ones) have chosen from the available variety of rules in order to present consolidated accounts in accordance with IASs.

6.3 In 1989, the IASC began a project to tighten its rules by removing many of the options in IASs. At the same time negotiations were begun with the International Organization of Securities Commissions (IOSCO), a group of governmental regulators of securities markets. The objectives of the negotiations is for IASC to produce a set of core standards which IOSCO can endorse as suitable for financial reporting by companies with cross-border listings.

6.4 In 1993, ten revised IASs were issued (in force from 1995). These met with some approval from IOSCO, but acceptance of the whole set of core standards now awaits further revised and new IASs, designed to be issued by 1998 or 1999. In the meantime IASs are the basis for standards in Hong Kong, Singapore and many Commonwealth countries, and they are used for group accounts by large multinationals in many other countries, such as Switzerland (and increasingly in Belgium, France and Germany).

6.5 A driving force here is the need for many large companies to gain access to world equity markets, which generally prefer the Anglo-American style of accounting, of which IASs are typical. At present, the Securities and Exchange Commission of the USA will not accept IASs for financial reporting by companies listed on US markets, but that might change in 1998/9. Meanwhile, a few Italian companies prepare reconciliations to US rules.

6.6 In France and Germany, the governments responded to these developments in 1996 by drafting laws allowing companies with foreign listings to depart from national laws for their group financial statements in order to follow IASC or US rules. The Belgian government is expected to follow this route, and the Italian government might do so.

6.7 In the 1990s, the IASC has been addressing increasingly complicated topics, such as financial instruments. The IASC is no longer always running behind national standard setters and is way in front of most European rule-makers. It has become clear that the EU harmonisation programme is too cumbersome to keep pace with these developments. In 1990, the EU said that these would be no more accounting Directives. In 1995, it abandoned plans for 'European Accounting Standards' and began to put its weight behind the IASC.

6.8 It seems that the IASC's influence in Europe is rapidly rising, particularly for group accounting by large companies. Accounting by individual companies seems to be little affected so far, and is still tied to tax and other legal rules in most countries. In the UK and the Netherlands, pressure will build up on the national standard setters to avoid differences from IASs. In other countries, large groups seeking international finance will be affected.

Appendix I

Formats

The compulsory or the most frequently found formats for financial statements are shown in the following pages. The lowest level of detail in the formats may generally be disclosed in the notes. The formats shown here are, in order of appearance:

1	UK	The vertical balance sheet used by the majority of companies.
2	UK	The most frequently used profit and loss account.
3	UK	The minority-used profit and loss account.
4	Belgium	The balance sheet.
5	Belgium	The profit and loss account (two-sided).
6	Italy	The balance sheet.
7	Italy	The profit and loss account.
8	Spain	The balance sheet.
9	Spain	The profit and loss account.

Formats

1 UK, balance sheet, format 1 (vertical)

Called up share capital not paid

Fixed assets
Intangible assets
    Development costs
    Concessions, patents, licences, trade marks and similar rights and assets
    Goodwill
    Payments on account

Tangible assets
    Land and buildings
    Plant and machinery
    Fixtures, fittings, tools and equipment
    Payments on account and assets in course of construction

Investments
    Shares in group undertakings
    Loans to group undertakings
    Interests in associated undertakings
    Other participating interests
    Other investments other than loans
    Other loans
    Own shares

Current assets
Stocks
    Raw materials and consumables
    Work in progress
    Finished goods and goods for resale
    Payments on account

Debtors
    Trade debtors
    Amounts owed by group undertakings
    Amounts owed by participating interests
    Other debtors
    Called up share capital not paid
    Prepayments and accrued income

Investments
    Shares in group undertakings
    Own shares
    Other investments

Cash at bank and in hand

Prepayments and accrued income

Creditors: amounts falling due within one year
Debenture loans
Bank loans and overdrafts
Payments received on account
Trade creditors
Bills of exchange payable
Amounts owed to group undertakings
Amounts owed to participating interests
Other creditors including taxation and social security
Accruals and deferred income

Net current assets (liabilities)

Total assets less current liabilities

Creditors: amounts falling due after more than one year
Debenture loans
Bank loans and overdrafts
Payments received on account
Trade creditors
Bills of exchange payable
Amounts owed to group undertakings
Amounts owed to participating interests
Other creditors including taxation and social security
Accruals and deferred income

Provisions for liabilities and charges
Pensions and similar obligations
Taxation, including deferred taxation
Other provisions

Accruals and deferred income

Minority interests

Capital and reserves
Called up share capital
Share premium account
Revaluation reserve
Other reserves
Capital redemption reserve
Reserve for own shares
Reserves provided for and by the articles of association
Other reserves
Profit and loss account

2 UK, profit and loss account, format 1

Turnover
Cost of sales
Gross profit or loss
Distribution costs
Administrative expenses
Other operating income
Income from interests in group undertakings
Income from interests in associated undertakings
Income from other participating interests
Income from other fixed asset investments
Other interest receivable and similar income
Amounts written off investments
Interest payable and similar charges
Profit or loss on ordinary activities before tax
Tax on profit or loss on ordinary activities
Profit or loss on ordinary activities after taxation
Profit or loss on ordinary activities attributable to minority interests
Extraordinary income
Extraordinary charges
Extraordinary profit or loss
Tax on extraordinary profit or loss
Profit or loss on extraordinary activities attributable to minority interests
Other taxes not shown under the above items
Profit or loss for the financial year

3 UK, profit and loss account, format 2

Turnover
Change in stocks of finished goods and in work in progress
Own work capitalised
Other operating income
Raw materials and consumables
Other external charges
Staff costs:
        (a) wages and salaries
        (b) social security costs
        (c) other pension costs
Depreciation and other amounts written off tangible and intangible fixed assets
Exceptional amounts written off current assets
Other operating charges
Income from shares in group undertakings
Income from shares in associated undertakings
Income from other fixed asset investments
Amounts written off investments
Interest payable and similar charges
Profit or loss on ordinary activities before tax
Tax on profit or loss on ordinary activities
Profit or loss on ordinary activities after taxation
Profit or loss on ordinary activities attributable to minority interests
Extraordinary income
Extraordinary charges
Extraordinary profit or loss
Profit or loss on ordinary activities before tax
Tax on extraordinary profit or loss
Profit or loss on extraordinary activities attributable to minority interests
Other taxes not shown under the above items
Profit or loss for the financial year

4 Belgium, balance sheet

Assets
Fixed assets
- I Formation expenses
- II Intangible assets
- III Tangible assets
  - A Land & buildings
  - B Plant, machinery & equipment
  - C Furniture & vehicles
  - D Leasing and other similar rights
  - E Other tangible assets
  - F Assets under construction and advance payments
- IV Financial assets
  - A Affiliated enterprises
    1. Investments
    2. Amounts receivable
  - B Other enterprises linked by participating interests
    1. Investments
    2. Amounts receivable
  - C Other financial assets
    1. Shares
    2. Amounts receivable and cash guarantees

Current assets
- V Amounts receivable after one year
  - A Trade debtors
  - B Other amounts receivable
- VI Stocks and contracts in progress
  - A Stocks
    1. Raw materials and consumables
    2. Work in progress
    3. Finished goods
    4. Goods purchased for resale
    5. Immovable property acquired or constructed for resale
    6. Advance payments
  - B Contracts in progress
- VII Amounts receivable within one year
  - A Trade debtors
  - B Other amounts receivable
- VIII Investments
  - A Own shares
  - B Other investments and deposits
- IX Cash at bank and in hand
- X Deferred charges and accrued income

Total assets

Liabilities
Capital and reserves
- I Capital
  - A Issues capital
  - B Uncalled capital (-)
- II Share premium account
- III Revaluation surplus
- IV Reserves
  - A Legal reserve
  - B Reserves not available for distribution
    1. In respect of own shares held
    2. Other
  - C Untaxed reserves
  - D Reserves available for distribution
- V Accumulated profits
  Accumulated losses (-)
- VI Investment grants

Provisions and deferred taxes
- VII
  - A Provisions for liabilities and charges
    1. Pensions and similar obligations
    2. Taxation
    3. Major repairs and maintenance
    4. Other liabilities and charges
  - B Deferred taxes

Liabilities
- VIII Amounts payable after one year
  - A Financial debts
    1. Subordinated loans
    2. Unsubordinated debentures
    3. Leasing and other similar obligations
    4. Credit institutions
    5. Other loans
  - B Trade debts
    1. Suppliers
    2. Bills of exchange payable
  - C Advances received on contracts in progress
  - D Other amounts payable
- IX Amounts payable within one year
  - A Current portion of amounts payable after one year
  - B Financial debts
    1. Credit institutions
    2. Other loans
  - C Trade debts
    1. Suppliers
    2. Bills of exchange payable
  - D Advances received on contracts in progress
  - E Taxes, remuneration and social security
    1. Taxes
    2. Remuneration and social security
  - F Other amounts payable
- X Accrued charges and deferred income

Total liabilities

Formats

5 Belgium, profit and loss account (two-sided)

Charges	Income

II Operating charges
  A Raw materials, consumables and goods for resale
    1 Purchases
    2 Increase (-); Decrease (+) in stocks
  B Services and other goods
  C Remuneration social security costs and pensions
  D Depreciation of and other amounts written off formation expenses, intangible and tangible fixed assets
  E Increase (+); Decrease (-) in amounts written off stocks, contracts in progress and trade debtors
  F Increase (+); Decrease (-) in provisions for liabilities and charges
  G Other operational charges
  H Operating charges capitalised under reorganisation costs (-)
V Financial charges
  A Interest and other debt charges
  B Increase (+): Decrease (-) in amounts written off current assets other than those mentioned under II E
  C Other financial charges
VIII Extraordinary charges
  A Extraordinary depreciation of and extraordinary amounts written off formation expenses, intangible and tangible fixed assets
  B Amounts written off financial fixed assets
  C Provisions for extraordinary liabilities and charges
  D Loss on disposal of fixed assets
  E Other extraordinary charges
  F Exceptional charges capitalised under reorganisation costs (-)
IX Transfer to deferred taxes
XA Income taxes
XI Profit for the year
    Total
XII Transfer to untaxed reserves
XIII Profit for the year available for appropriation
	I Operating income
	  A Turnover
	  B Increase (+); Decrease (-) in stocks of finished goods, work and contracts in progress
	  C Fixed assets – own construction
	  D Other operating income
	IV Financial income
	  A Income from financial fixed assets
	  B Income from current assets
	  C Other financial income
	VII Extraordinary income
	  A Adjustments to depreciation of and to other amounts written off intangible and tangible fixed assets
	  B Adjustments to amounts written off financial fixed assets
	  C Adjustments to provisions for extraordinary liabilities and charges
	  D Gain on disposal of fixed assets
	  E Other extraordinary income
	IX Transfer from deferred taxes
	XB Adjustment of income taxes and write-back of tax provisions
	XI Loss for the year
	XII Transfer from untaxed reserves
	    Total
	XIII Loss for the year transferred to appropriation account

6 Italy, balance sheet

Assets

A Called up share capital not paid

B Fixed Assets

   I Intangible assets

   II Tangible assets

   III Investments

C Current assets

   I Stocks

   II Debtors

   III Financial assets other than long-term

   IV Cash at bank and in hand

D Prepayments and accrued income

Shareholders' fund and liabilities

A Shareholders' capital

   I Called up share capital

   II Share premium account

   III Revaluation reserve

   IV Legal reserve

   V Reserve for own shares

   VI Reserves provided for by the articles

   VII Other reserves, specifically identified

   VIII Profits (losses) of previous years

   IX Profit (loss) for the year

B Provisions for risks and liabilities

C Statutory provisions for severance indemnities

D Creditors

E Accruals and deferred income

Formats

7 Italy, profit and loss account

A Value of production (ordinary operations)
    1 Turnover
    2 Change in stocks of finished goods and work in progress
    3 Change in long-term contract stocks
    4 Other work capitalised
    5 Other ordinary income

B Production costs (ordinary operations)
    6 Raw materials and consumables
    7 External services
    8 Rents
    9 Staff costs
        (a) wages and salaries
        (b) social security costs
        (c) statutory severance costs
        (d) other pension costs and similar
        (e) other costs
   10 Depreciation and write-offs
        (a) depreciation of intangible assets
        (b) depreciation of tangible assets
        (c) other amounts written off from fixed assets
        (d) amounts written off from current debtors and from liquid funds
   11 Change in stocks of raw materials and consumables
   12 Provision for risks
   13 Other provisions
   14 Other operating charges

A-B Difference between production value and costs

C Income and charges from financial assets
   15 Income from participating interests
   16 Other income from financial assets
        (a) Income from debtors under fixed assets
        (b) Income from fixed asset investments other than participating interests
        (c) Income from current asset investments other than participating interests
        (d) Other income
   17 Interest payable and similar charges

D Changes in value of financial assets
   18 Revaluations
        (a) of participating interests
        (b) of fixed asset investments other than (a)
        (c) of current asset investments other than (a)
   19 Write-offs
      a-c (as above)

E Extraordinary income and charges
   20 Extraordinary income
   21 Extraordinary charges

Profit or loss before taxation
    22 Tax on profit
    23 Profit or loss for the financial year

8   Spain, balance sheet*

Assets

A   Share capital not called

B   Fixed assets

    I   Formation expenses

    II   Intangible assets

    III Tangible assets

    IV   Financial assets

C   Current assets

    I   Called up share capital not paid

    II   Stocks

    III Debtors

    IV   Marketable securities

    V   Cash and bank

    VI   Prepayments and accrued income

Capital and liabilities

A   Equity capital

    I   Issued capital

    II   Share premium

    III Revaluation reserve

    IV   Reserves

    V   Results of earlier years

    VI   Results of this year

B   Provisions for risks and charges

C   Long-term creditors

D   Short-term creditors

*   The balance sheet in the law is shown with these headings. However, the balance sheet in the General Accounting Plan (which has the force of law) requires also the next level of detail for long-term and short-term creditors to be shown on the face of the balance sheet (except for small companies). The next level of detail is much the same as in other EU countries, but is dealt with separately in the law. This lowest level need not be shown on the face of the balance sheet or, for small companies, need not be shown at all.

9 Spain, profit and loss account

A Expenses

1 Decrease in stocks of finished goods and work in progress

2 (a) Consumption of raw materials and other consumables
   (b) Other external charges

3 Personnel costs
   (a) Wages, salaries and similar
   (b) Social security, pensions

4 (a) Depreciation and provisions for fixed assets
   (b) Provisions for current assets

5 Other operating costs

6 Depreciation and provisions for financial fixed assets and marketable securities

7 Interest and similar expenses

8 Result on ordinary activities

9 Extraordinary expenses

10 Corporation tax

11 Other taxes

12 Result

B Revenues

1 Sales

2 Increase in stocks of finished goods and work in progress

3 Own work capitalised

4 Other operating income

5 Income from participations

6 Income from other investments

7 Interest and similar income

8 Result on ordinary activities

9 Extraordinary income

10 Result

Appendix II

Glossary

The terms that follow are shown in the order: English, French, Italian and Spanish. Readers who wish to find the German and Dutch equivalents should consult *Accounting Comparisons: UK, Netherlands, France and Germany*. Coopers & Lybrand also publish the *Diccionario de Informes Financieros Inglés-Español* providing authoritative translations for all terms in English/Spanish financial reporting.

Glossary

English	French
A	
account	poste (bookkeeping), compte (eg bank)
accountancy, accounting	comptabilité
accountant	comptable
accounts (annual)	comptes annuels
accruals	comptes de regularisation, charge à payer (liability)
additions (fixed assets)	investissements
annual general meeting	assemblée générale ordinaire
appropriation	affectation
articles (of limited company)	statuts
assets	éléments de l'actif
associated company	participation
audit	audit, révision
auditor	commissaire
authorised capital	capital autorisé
B	
balance (on an account)	solde
balance sheet	bilan
bank	banque
bearer (share)	action au porteur
bill of exchange	effet
board of directors	conseil d'administration
bonus issue	émission d'actions gratuites
bookkeeping	comptabilité, tenue des livres comptables
books of account	livres comptables

Glossary

Italian	Spanish
conto	cuenta
ragioneria, contabilità	contabilidad
contabile	contable (also bookkeeper), experto
bilancio	cuentas anuales
accantonamenti	ajustes por periodificación, pagos diferidos
incrementi	compras
assemblea annuale degli azionisti	junta general de accionistas
stanziamento	distribución
statuto	estatutos
attività	activos
consociata, collegata	compañía asociada
revisione contabile	auditoría
revisore, sindaco (statutory)	auditor
capitale autorizzato, approvato	capital autorizado
saldo	saldo
stato patrimoniale	balance de situación, balance
banca	banco
azione al portatore	acción al portador
cambiale, effetto	letra de cambio
consiglio d'amministrazione	consejo de administración
emissione d'azioni gratuite	emisión de acciones liberadas
contabilità	teneduría de libros
libri contabili	libros contables

Glossary

English	French
B (continued)	
borrowings	endettements (total), emprunt (loan payable)
buildings	bâtiments, constructions, immeubles
business	affaires
C	
capital	capital
capital employed	capitaux propres
capital gain	plus-value
capital loss	moins-value
capitalise (expenses to assets)	porter à l'actif
cash at bank	valeurs disponibles
cash in hand, cash	caisse
cash flow	cash flow, autofinancement
chairman	président, PDG
chartered accountant	expert comptable (equivalent)
cheque	chèque
Civil Code	Code Civil
Commercial Code	Code de Commerce
company	société
consolidated	consolidé
contingent	éventuel
contract	contrat, convention
conversion	conversion (convertible debentures, foreign currencies)
convertible	convertible

Italian

finanziamenti, prestiti

fabbricati

affari

capitale sociale
(no equivalent)
plusvalenza
minusvalenza
capitalizzare
liquido in banca
cassa, liquido in cassa
cash flow
presidente
dottore commercialista (nearest equivalent)
assegno
codice civile
(no equivalent)
società
consolidato
potenziale
contratto
cambio, conversione
 (of foreign currency)

convertibile

Spanish

endeudamiento, préstamos

edificios

negocios

capital
financiación básica
plusvalía
minusvalía
capitalizar, activar
saldo bancario
efectivo
cash flow
presidente
censor jurado de cuentas
 (nearest equivalent)
talón, cheque
Código Civil
Código de Comercio
sociedad, compañía, firma
consolidado
contingente
contrato, convenio
cambio

convertible

Glossary

English	French
C (continued)	
corporation tax	impôt sur les sociétés
cost (purchase cost)	coût, prix de revient, prix d'achat (purchase cost)
cost accounting	comptabilité analytique
costs	frais, charges
credit	passif (balance sheet), avoir (bookkeeping), crédit
creditor	créancier, créditeur
currency	devise
current assets	valeurs d'exploration + valeurs réalisables à court terme et disponibles
current value	valeur actuelle
current liabilities	dettes à court terme
D	
debenture	obligation
debit	doit, débit (bookkeeping), actif (balance sheet)
debt	créance (not *dette* = liability)
debtor	débiteur
deductible	déductible
deferred charge, deferred credit	charge à reporter
deferred tax provision	provision pour impôt différé
depreciation	amortissements (provision), dotation aux comptes d'amortissements (charge)

| **Italian** | **Spanish** |

imposta sul reddito delle
  persone giuridiche (IRPEG)
costo

contabilità industriale

spese, costi
passività (balance sheet), avere
  (bookkeeping), credito
fornitore, creditore
moneta (valuta)
attività correnti

valore corrente
passività correnti

obbligazione
dare (bookkeeping), attività
  (balance sheet)
prestito
credito, debitore
deducibile
oneri pluriannali, spese
  differite
imposte differite
ammortamento

impuesto sobre sociedades

coste

contabilidad analítica,
  contabilidad de costes,
  contabilidad industrial
costes, gastos
pasivo (balance sheet), haber
  (bookkeeping), crédito
acreedor
divisa, moneda
activo circulante, activo corriente

valor actual
pasivo circulante, corriente

obligación
debe (bookkeeping), activo
  (balance sheet)
préstamos, deuda
deudor
deducible
gasto diferido, ingreso
  diferido
provisión por impuesto diferido
depreciación, amortización

Glossary

English	French
D (continued)	
director	administrateur
discount	prime de remboursement, remettre à l'escompte (bills of exchange)
disposal (fixed assets)	cession d'actif
distribution (dividend)	répartition
dividend	dividende
doubtful debts	créances douteuses
due	échu (bills of exchange), exigible (other debts)
E	
employee	l'effectif, salariés
exceptional	exceptionnel
exchange (foreign)	change
exchange rate	taux de change
expenditure, expenses	charges, dépenses
exports	exportations
extraordinary	exceptionnel
F	
factory	usine
figure	chiffre
finished goods	produits, finis
fixed assets	immobilisations
fixed costs	frais fixes
fixtures and fittings	agencements, aménagements, installations

Italian	**Spanish**
amministratore	consejero, administrador
sconti, abbuoni di vendita	descuento
cessione, vendita	venta, baja, enajenación
distribuzione	distribución, reparto
dividendo	dividendo
crediti dubbi	deudores morosos, saldos dudosos
dovuto	vencido
dipendente	empleado
straordinaria	extraordinario
cambio	cambio
tasso di cambio	tipo de cambio
spese	gasto
esportazione	exportaciones
straordinario	extraordinario
fabbrica, stabilimento	fábrica
cifra	cifra
prodotti finiti	productos terminados
immobili, beni patrimoniali	activos fijos, inmovilizado material
costi fissi	gastos fijos
arredi	mobiliario y enseres

Glossary

English	French
F (continued)	
furniture	mobilier, meubles
G	
gearing	ratio d'endettement
general reserve	réserve général
goods	marchandises
goodwill	fonds de commerce
gross	brut
group	groupe
guarantee	garantie (for goods sold), caution (for third party's debts)
H	
hire	louer
holding company	société mère
I	
income	revenue
income tax	impôt sur le revenue
indirect costs	frais indirects, frais généraux
insurance	assurance
intangibles	immobilisations incorporelles
interest	intérêts
interim dividend	acompte sur dividendes
interim report	rapport intérimaire
investments	investissements (in fixed assets)

Glossary

Italian	**Spanish**

Italian	Spanish
mobili	mobiliario, muebles
gearing	apalancamiento
riserva disponibile	reserva voluntaria
merci	bienes, mercancías, productos
avviamento	fondo de comercio
lordo	bruto
gruppo	grupo
garanzia	garantía
noleggiare	alquilar
casa madre	dominante, matriz, holding
utile, reddito, ricavi	ingreso, renta
imposte	impuesto sobre la renta
costi indiretti	costes indirectos
assicurazione	seguro
intangibili, immoblizzazioni immateriali	intangibles, immovilizado intangible
interesse	interés
acconto dividendo	dividendo activo a cuenta
rapporto semestrale	informe interino
investimenti	inmovilizado financiero (securities), inversiones

Glossary

English	French
L	
land	terrains
law	loi
lease	bail, crédit-bail (leasing agreement)
liabilities	dettes
limited company	société anonyme (public), société à responsabilité, limitée (private)
limited partnership (with share certificates)	société en commandite (par actions)
liquidity	liquidité
loans	emprunt (payable), prêt (receivable)
loan capital	obligation
long term	à long terme
loss	perte
M	
machinery	machines, matériel
manager	gérant (SARL); directeur (SA, ie not on board)
managing director	directeur général
market value	au cours du marché, au cours du jour
merger	fusion
minorities	intérêts minoritaires
minutes	procès-verbal
money	argent
mortgage	hypothèque

Italian	Spanish
terreni	terrenos
legge	ley
leasing	arrendamiento financiero
passività	deudas (creditors), pasivo (balance sheet)
società per azioni (public), società a responsabilità limitata (private)	sociedad anónima (SA) (public), sociedad limitada (SL) (private)
società in accomandita (per azioni)	sociedad en comandita (por acciones)
liquidità	liquidez
prestiti	empréstitos, préstamos
prestiti a lungo termine	préstamos a largo plazo
a lungo termine	a largo plazo
perdita	pérdida
macchinario	maquinaria
direttore, dirigente	gerente
amministratore delegato	director gerente
prezzo di mercato	valor de mercado
fusione	fusión
minoranza	minoritarios
verbali	actas
denaro	moneda, dinero
ipoteca	hipoteca

Glossary

English	French
M (continued)	
motor vehicles	matériel de transport
N	
net	net
nominal	nominal
notes to the accounts	notes, commentaire, explications, annexe
O	
office	bureau
ordinary share	action
overheads	frais généraux
P	
paid up, fully paid	libéré
par	nominale
partnership	association
patent	brevet
pay, payable, paid	payer, à payer, payé
pension	pension
pension fund	caisse de retraite
p/e ratio	rapport cours/bénéfice
personnel	personnel, effectif
plant	matériel
preference shares	actions preferentielles
preliminary expenses	frais de constitution
premium	prime
prepayments	compte de régularisation actif, avance (on order etc.)

Italian

autoveicoli

netto
nominale
note esplicative

ufficio
azione ordinaria
spese generali

sottoscritto e versato
nominale
società in nome colletivo

brevetto
pagare, pagabile. pagato
pensione
fundo pensione
p/e ratio
personale
impianti e macchinari
azioni privilegiate
spese di costituzione
somma addizionale, premio
risconti attivi

Spanish

automóviles, vehículos

neto
nominal
memoria

oficina
acción ordinaria
gastos generales

desembolsado
nominal
sociedad en comandita, sociedad
  comanditaria
patente
pagar, a pagar, pagado
pensión
fondo de pensiones
PER
personal
instalaciones
acciones preferentes
gastos de primer establecimiento
prima
gastos anticipados

English

P (continued)
price
prior period
private company

profit
profitability
profit and loss account

production
provision
proxy
public company
purchase

Q
quoted

R
rate (eg depr.)
raw materials
realisable value
receipt

redemption
reducing balance (depreciation)
registered office
registered (share)

French

prix
exercise antérieur
société à responsabilité
   limitée
bénéfice, profit
rentabilité
compte de resultats

production, fabrication
provision
formule de procuration
société anonyme (SA)
acheter (verb), achats de
   matières et marchandises
   (noun)

admis à la côte officielle d'une
   bourse de valeurs

taux
matières premières
la valeur probable de réalisation
quittance (piece of paper),
   recette
remboursement
amortissement dégressif
siège social
action nominative

Italian	Spanish
prezzo	precio
esercizio precedente	ejercicio anterior
società a responsabilità limitata	sociedad de responsabilidad limitada
utile	beneficio, ganancia
profitabilità	rentabilidad
conto perdite e profitti, conto economico	cuenta de pérdidas y ganancias, cuenta de resultados
produzione	producción
fondo	provisión
procura	poder
società per azioni	sociedad anónima
comprare, aquisto	comprar, compra
quotato	cotizado, con cotización oficial
tasso	tasa, tipo
materie prime	materias primas
valore realizzabile	valor de realización
ricevuta, quietanza	recibo
riscatto	cancelación, amortización
a saldi decrescenti	amortización degresiva
domicilio legale, sede legale	domicilio social, sede social
registrato	acción nominativa

Glossary

English	French
R (continued)	
rent out, let	donner en location
remuneration	rémunération
replacement cost	coût de remplacement
report	rapport
report and accounts	plaquette annuelle, rapport annuel
research and development	recherche et développement
reserve	réserve
results	résultats
retained earnings	report à nouveau + any free reserves
revaluation	réévaluation
revenue	revenu, produits
royalty	redevance
S	
salary	appointments
sale, sell	vente, vendre
security	sûreté (on loan), valeur mobilière (shares)
share	action (SA), part (SARL, partnership)
share capital	capital social
shareholder	actionnaire
shareholders' funds	situation nette, fondes propres
share premium	prime d'émission (paid for in cash), prime de fusion (on merger), prime d'apport (paid for in assets)
shop	magasin

Italian	**Spanish**
affittare	alquilar
stipendio, emolumento	remuneración
costo di sostituzione	coste de reposición
rapporto	informe
rapporto e bilancio	cuentas anuales e informe de gestión
ricerca e sviluppo	investigación y desarrollo
riserva	reserva
resultati	resultados
utili non distribuiti	beneficios retenidos, reservas
rivalutazione	revaluación
ricavi	ingresos
diritto, royalty	royalty
stipendio	sueldo
vendita, vendere	venta, vender
garancia (loan), titoli (shares)	garantía (loan), valor, acción (shares)
azione	acción, participatión
capitale sociale	capital social
azionista	accionista
partrimonio netto	fondos propios, patrimonio neto
fondo sovraprezza azioni	prima de emisión
magazzino, negozio	tienda

Glossary

English	French
S (continued)	
short term	court terme
solvency	solvabilité
source and application of funds	ressources et emplois des fonds, tableau de financement (statement)
start-up costs	frais de démarrage
stocks (inventories)	stocks, valeurs d'exploitation
stock exchange	bourse
stocktaking	prise d'inventaire, inventaire physique
straight line (depreciation)	linéaire
subsidiary	filiale
sundry	autres, divers
supervisory board	conseil de surveillance
T	
takeover bid	offre publique d'achat (cash), offre publique d'échange (securities)
tax	impôt, taxe
tools	outils
trade mark	brevet
trade union	syndicat
trading profit	profit d'exploitation
transfer	dotation (to provisions), reprise (from provisions), prélèvement (from reserves)
translation (currency)	conversion
turnover	chiffre d'affaires, ventes

Italian	Spanish
a breve termine	a corto plazo
liquidità, solvabilità	solvencia
rendiconto finanziario	origen y aplicación de fondos, cuadro de financiación (statement)
spese preliminari	gastos de establecimiento
rimanenze di magazzino, inventario	existencias, stock
borsa valori	bolsa de comercio
inventario fisico	recuento físico, toma de inventario
a quote costanti	línea recta
società controllata	dependiente, filial, subsidiaria
diversi	varios
(no direct equivalent)	(no direct equivalent)
scalata	OPA
imposta	impuesto
attrezzature	herramientas, utillaje
marchio	marca
sindicato	sindicato
utile operativo	beneficio de explotación
trasferimento	transferencia, dotación (to provisions or reserves)
conversione	conversión
fatturato	cifra de negocios

Glossary

English	French
U	
unquoted	non admis á la côte officielle d'une bourse de valeurs
V	
valuation	évaluation
value	valeur
value added tax (VAT)	taxe sur la valeur ajoutée (TVA)
variable	variable
variance	écart
W	
wages	salaires
withholding tax	retenue à la source
working capital	fonds de roulement
work in progress	produits ou travaux en cours
works council	comité d'entreprise
Y	
yield	rendement

Italian	Spanish
non quotata	sin cotización
valutazione	valoración
valore	valor
imposta sul valore aggiunto (IVA)	impuesto sobre el valor añadido (IVA)
variabile	variable
varianza	desviación
retribuzioni, salari	salarios
ritenuta d'acconto	impuesto retenido, retención
capitale circolante	capital circulante
lavoro in corso	productos en curso
(no direct equivalent)	comité de empresa
rendimento	rentabilidad, rendimento